POLISH
COOKING

Rose Cantrell

WEATHERVANE
BOOKS

contents

introduction

Polish cooking is as diverse and interesting as Poland's political history. Beginning in the eleventh century, to as recently as World War II, Poland has been bartered, sold, or lost by its reigning ruler, or lost in battle to its neighboring countries.

Each new ruler or government brought with it the cuisine of his mother country, and it was adopted by the wealthy class and the lower echelons of government, wanting to maintain their power. Today Polish cuisine is ranked by gourmet diners next to or above the cuisine served in France.

It would be misleading to the reader to say that the entire Polish population has access to this wide variety of food, since the majority of the Polish population is comprised of farmers who live off the land. They have a limited amount of cash with which to purchase many of the ingredients of the foods served in the restaurants of Warsaw.

The diet of the rural Polish citizen consists of foods produced on their farms and wild game and fish caught from the many streams that wind through the Polish countryside.

No matter where you dine in Poland—in Warsaw or with a farm family—the experience will be one you will remember for a long time. Eating is an integral part of Polish hospitality. The traditional meal starts with a hearty appetizer while you sit around the large family table and visit. Next comes the main part of the meal, consisting of a salad, one or two main dishes, potatoes or dumplings, two or three vegetables, and a hot bread and butter. The evening would end with lively conversation, freshly brewed strong coffee topped with whipped cream, and a rich dessert.

The intent of this cookbook is to provide the reader and chef with a cross section of the cuisine found in the finest restaurant in Warsaw and that found on rural farms.

appetizers

quark snacks

2 cups all-purpose white flour
3 teaspoons baking powder
1 teaspoon salt
¼ cup all-vegetable shortening
¾ cup milk (about)
2 egg yolks, beaten
3 tablespoons caraway seeds

cottage-cheese filling
1 cup dry-curd cottage cheese
2 tablespoons dried parsley flakes
1 teaspoon salt
2 tablespoons chopped pimiento

Combine dry ingredients; cut in shortening to resemble a coarse meal. Add milk to form a soft dough. Knead dough 6 times. Roll dough on floured surface to ¼ inch thickness. Brush half the biscuits with beaten egg yolks; sprinkle with caraway seeds.

Bake biscuits at 450°F for 10 minutes or until golden brown.

Make Cottage-Cheese Filling by combining cottage cheese, parsley flakes, salt, and pimiento.

To serve, spread Cottage-Cheese Filling on plain biscuits and top with caraway-seed biscuits. Makes 20 snacks.

Picture on next page: quark snacks

cream-cheese spread

1 3-ounce package cream cheese
1 cup small-curd cottage cheese
½ teaspoon caraway seeds
1 teaspoon capers
1 tablespoon minced onion
1 loaf party rye bread

Soften cream cheese; place in blender. Add remaining ingredients; blend. Chill thoroughly.

To serve, spread on party rye bread slices. Makes 12 servings.

pickled herrings

2 pounds salt herring
2 cups water
⅓ cup cider vinegar
1 medium onion, sliced into rings
¼ cup granulated sugar
1 teaspoon pickling spices
½ teaspoon mustard seed

Skin herring; remove backbone. Cut fish into 1- to 2-inch pieces. Soak fish in cold water overnight to remove salt.

Next morning drain water from fish; rinse fish in cold water.

Combine remaining ingredients; pour over herring. Marinate fish overnight in refrigerator.

Serve herrings chilled. Makes approximately 1 quart.

shrimp paste

½ cup cooked shrimp
2 tablespoons chili sauce
2 tablespoons mayonnaise
2 tablespoons lemon juice
¼ teaspoon dillweed

Place ingredients in blender. Cover; blend for 30 seconds, scraping sides once during blending process.

Serve with crackers. Makes ¾ cup.

stuffed mushroom caps

24 fresh mushroom caps
⅔ cup mayonnaise
¼ cup Parmesan cheese
¼ teaspoon garlic powder

Wash mushroom caps; let dry on a paper towel.

Combine mayonnaise, cheese, and garlic powder. Mix well.

Fill mushroom caps with cheese mixture; place under broiler 4 inches from flame. Broil approximately 5 minutes, or until cheese melts and mixture is golden brown and bubbly. Makes 24 mushroom caps.

cabbage dunking bowl

1 small cabbage head
1 cup mayonnaise
1 tablespoon minced onion
1 tablespoon finely chopped Bread-and-Butter
   Pickles (see Index)
1 tablespoon anchovy paste
¼ teaspoon salt
¼ teaspoon white pepper

Clean and wash cabbage head. Hollow out center of cabbage for dip. Refrigerate until ready to serve.

Put remaining ingredients into blender; blend.

Fill hollowed-out cabbage head with dip just before serving. Makes 1 cup.

blue-cheese dip

Delicious served with potato chips.

1 ounce blue cheese
1 cup small-curd cottage cheese
¼ cup minced onions
¼ cup sour cream

Crumble blue cheese into cottage cheese; blend. Pour cheese mixture into blender, add remaining ingredients, and blend.

Chill before serving. Makes 1¼ cups.

deviled crayfish dip

½ cup crayfish meat
2 hard-cooked eggs
¼ teaspoon salt
⅛ teaspoon white pepper
2 tablespoons lemon juice
½ cup mayonnaise
1 sprig parsley

Chop crayfish and eggs. Add remaining ingredients (except parsley) to crayfish and egg mixture; blend. Chill.

Serve garnished with parsley. Makes 1 cup.

green-olive dip

6 ounces cream cheese
½ cup green-olive meat
¼ cup milk
¼ teaspoon salt
¼ teaspoon white pepper

Soften cream cheese; add remaining ingredients. Blend well. If dip is too thick, more milk may be added to obtain desired consistency. Makes 1 cup.

egg and parsley dip

8 hard-cooked egg yolks
1 tablespoon crushed parsley flakes
2 tablespoons wine vinegar
1 tablespoon minced onion
½ teaspoon seasoned salt
¼ teaspoon white pepper
¼ teaspoon dillweed
½ cup mayonnaise

Mash egg yolks. Add remaining ingredients to mashed egg yolks; blend well.
Refrigerate before serving. Makes ¾ cup.

mushroom and chicken-liver dip

½ pound chicken livers
¼ cup butter
1 3-ounce can mushroom stems and pieces
2 tablespoons minced onion
2 tablespoons chopped parsley
½ cup mayonnaise
½ teaspoon salt
¼ teaspoon white pepper

Sauté livers in butter until brown. Drain; chop fine.
Drain and chop mushrooms. Add to chicken livers. Add remaining ingredients; blend well. Makes 1½ cups.

mixed-vegetable dip

¼ cup minced pimiento
¼ cup minced parsley
¼ cup minced onion
¼ cup minced green pepper
¼ teaspoon salt
¼ teaspoon garlic powder
2 hard-cooked egg yolks, mashed
½ cup mayonnaise

Combine all ingredients. Chill until ready to serve. Makes 1¼ cups.

sour-cream dip

A delicious vegetable dip.

1 cup sour cream
1 teaspoon prepared horseradish (more, if desired)
¼ teaspoon celery seed

Combine ingredients; mix well. Chill well before serving. Makes 1 cup.

9

chilled apricot soup

A quick fruit soup for an impromptu dinner party.

2 No. 2½ cans apricot halves
1 cup sour cream

Chill apricot halves thoroughly. Drain.

Blend drained apricot halves in blender. Add sour cream; continue to blend until well-mixed. Serve chilled. Makes 4 servings.

sour-cream peach soup

2 No. 303 cans peaches, sliced
1¾ cups peach juice and cold water
1 tablespoon cornstarch
1 teaspoon lemon juice
⅔ cup sour cream
½ teaspoon cinnamon (if desired)

Drain peaches; reserve liquid. Puree peaches. Set aside.

Measure drained peach liquid. Add enough cold water to equal 1¾ cups liquid.

Thicken ¼ cup peach juice and water with cornstarch. Add thickened juice to remaining liquid; heat until thickened, about 10 minutes. Stir in lemon juice. Add pureed peaches and sour cream; blend well. Serve immediately.

If desired, garnish with cinnamon before serving. Makes 4 servings.

polish eggs in the shell

4 hard-cooked eggs in the shells
½ bunch parsley, chopped fine
3 tablespoons butter
1 teaspoon salt
1 teaspoon paprika
¼ cup shredded Muenster cheese

Cut eggs in half with large, sharp knife; scoop eggs out of shells. Save shells. Chop egg whites fine; squeeze yolks fine with a fork.

Combine chopped eggs, parsley, butter, salt, and paprika. Mix well. Refill egg shells with egg mixture. Sprinkle with cheese. Bake 10 minutes at 400°F or until cheese melts and browns. Makes 4 servings.

polish eggs in the shell

steak with mushroom caps

A delicious brunch dish.

1 teaspoon salt
½ teaspoon black pepper, peppermill-ground
4 2-ounce fillets mignons
¼ cup butter
1 cup fresh mushroom caps
¼ cup mayonnaise
2 teaspoons horseradish
4 slices toast
4 lemon slices
Dillweed

Salt and pepper both sides of fillets.

Melt butter in heavy skillet. Sauté steaks to desired doneness. Remove from skillet; add mushrooms. Sauté mushrooms until done.

Combine mayonnaise and horseradish. Spread each toast slice with mixture.

To serve, place steaks on toast slices and top each steak with ¼ cup mushrooms. Garnish with lemon slice and dillweed. Makes 4 servings.

Picture on next page: steak with mushroom caps

11

polish links

1½ cups all-purpose white flour
3-ounce package cream cheese, softened
½ cup butter
6 Polish links
1 egg yolk, beaten

Combine flour, cream cheese, and butter; mix until a soft dough forms. Divide dough into 7 equal parts. Wrap each link in dough.

Cut remaining dough into crescent shapes. Place crescents on top of wrapped Polish links; press to secure. Brush each wrapped link with beaten egg yolk. Bake in 425°F oven 10 to 12 minutes or until golden brown.

Slice to serve. Makes 6 servings.

polish links

salads

spiced apple salad

1 cup granulated sugar
1 cup cold water
1 cup red hots (red cinnamon candies)
6 tart medium apples
1 cup creamed cottage cheese, small curd
½ cup finely chopped English walnuts
12 large lettuce leaves

Combine sugar, water, and cinnamon candies in saucepan. Cook over low heat until candy dissolves.

Pare and core apples. Place them in the syrup; cover and cook very slowly until apples are tender but not broken. Turn apples serveral times during cooking period, so they will be even in color. Remove apples from syrup; drain and chill them thoroughly.

Mix cottage cheese and walnuts. Fill apple centers with cheese and nut mixture.

To serve, arrange filled apples on lettuce beds. Makes 6 servings.

bacon and spinach salad bowl

8 slices bacon
1 pound raw spinach
3 hard-cooked eggs, chopped fine
2 tablespoons minced parsley

Fry bacon until crisp. Drain bacon on brown paper bag; crumble.

Tear spinach into bite-size pieces; place in salad bowl. Add bacon pieces and chopped eggs; toss lightly.

Serve salad with your favorite dressing. Makes 6 servings.

beet and pickle salad

2 cups cooked sliced beets
½ cup beet juice
½ cup bread-and-butter pickle juice
1 cup Bread-and-Butter Pickles (see Index)
¼ cup mayonnaise

Place beets, beet juice, and pickle juice in saucepan. Cover pan; simmer beets for 30 minutes. Remove from heat; add Bread-and-Butter Pickles. Chill mixture 24 hours.

To serve salad, drain and place in individual salad bowls; garnish with mayonnaise. Makes 6 servings.

eggs stuffed with mushrooms

6 hard-cooked eggs
¼ teaspoon salt
½ teaspoon prepared mustard
½ teaspoon lemon juice
1 tablespoon mayonnaise
¼ teaspoon white pepper
1 3-ounce can mushroom stems and pieces
2 tablespoons chopped pimiento

Peel, halve, and place yolks in a bowl. Mash yolks until smooth. Add salt, mustard, lemon juice, mayonnaise, and white pepper. Mix well.

Drain and chop mushrooms. Add mushrooms to egg-yolk mixture; mix well.

Fill egg whites with egg-yolk and mushroom mixture; garnish each filled egg half with chopped pimiento. Makes 6 servings.

15

pickled eggs

To give your dishes a different taste, use pickled eggs in place of hard-cooked eggs in your recipes.

1 quart water
½ cup granulated sugar
1 cup cider vinegar
1 teaspoon salt
1 tablespoon pickling spices
12 eggs

Combine water, sugar, vinegar, salt, and pickling spices. Bring to a rolling boil. Cook for 10 minutes. Cool to room temperature.

Hard-cook eggs. Peel and place them into a large container with a cover. Add cooled brine; marinate for 2 to 7 days, depending on taste preference. Makes 12 eggs.

red eggs

6 eggs
1 quart juice from pickled beets

Hard cook eggs. Peel and place in large container with a cover. Add pickled-beet juice; marinate for 24 to 48 hours, depending on taste preference. Makes 6 pickled red eggs.

bread-and-butter pickles

The Polish growing season is very short. To utilize the precious garden produce, delicious pickle recipes are the prized possessions of Polish cooks.

2½ gallons cucumbers, unpeeled
   and sliced paper-thin
2 large Spanish onions, peeled
   and sliced paper-thin
3 large sweet green peppers, cleaned and
   sliced into paper-thin strips
¼ cup pickling salt*
4 cups cider vinegar
4 cups granulated sugar
2 tablespoons mustard seed
1½ teaspoons turmeric
½ teaspoon whole cloves

In a 6-gallon container layer cucumbers, onions, green peppers, and pickling salt. Cover with crushed ice; let stand 4 hours. Drain; rinse in ice-cold water.

Combine vinegar, sugar, mustard seed, turmeric, and cloves to form pickling brine. Stir to dissolve sugar. Bring pickling brine to a boil. Add drained vegetables; again bring mixture to a boil. Remove from heat immediately. Pack vegetables into sterilized pint jars. Cover with pickling brine to ½ inch from jar rim. Seal jars; process in a boiling-water bath for 15 minutes. Makes 12 pints.

*Do not use table salt; it will make your pickling brine cloudy.

cottage-cheese-stuffed tomatoes

A quick main dish for a hot summer day.

4 large tomatoes
½ teaspoon salt
1 cup small-curd cottage cheese
½ cup tomato pulp
¼ cup minced onions
4 sprigs parsley

Wash and peel tomatoes. Remove cores, cut into quarters almost to the base, and spread apart. Salt tomatoes. Chill them thoroughly.

Mix cottage cheese with tomato pulp and minced onions.

To serve, fill tomatoes with cottage-cheese and vegetable mixture. Garnish with parsley. Makes 4 servings.

cauliflower and green-pepper mix

1 small head cauliflower, sliced thin
½ cup thinly sliced green pepper
¼ cup diced celery hearts
1 teaspoon salt
1 cup commercial French dressing
8 lettuce cups

Gently toss cauliflower, green pepper, and celery hearts.

Combine salt and French dressing; pour over mixed vegetables. Mix well. Chill and marinate salad 2 hours.

To serve, arrange lettuce cups on salad plates and fill each cup with salad mixture. Makes 8 servings.

dilled croutons

A delicious and economical addition to a tossed salad.

1-pound loaf day-old bread
1 cup butter
2 teaspoons onion salt
2 tablespoons dried parsley flakes
1 teaspoon dried dillweed

Cube bread into ½-inch cubes. Spread cubes evenly over a cookie sheet; let dry for 2 days or until cubes lose their moisture and become hard.

Melt butter in large skillet. Remove butter from skillet; reserve. Add onion salt, parsley flakes, and dillweed to melted butter. Mix well.

Reheat skillet in which butter was melted. Add croutons; distribute evenly over skillet surface. Pour melted-butter mixture over croutons. Stir to distribute evenly. Fry croutons until golden brown and heated thoroughly. Cool. Store up to 1 month in airtight container. Makes 2 quarts.

cucumbers in
dill vinegar

4 small cucumbers (pickling size)
1 teaspoon salt

dill vinegar
¼ teaspoon dillweed
¼ teaspoon white pepper
¼ cup cider vinegar
½ cup cold water

Wash and slice cucumbers into thin circles. *Do not peel.* Place cucumbers in shallow serving dish; sprinkle with salt. Stir cucumbers to distribute salt evenly over surfaces of slices. Let set 1 hour.

Prepare Dill Vinegar by combining dillweed, pepper, vinegar, and cold water.

Pour Dill Vinegar over salted cucumbers. Refrigerate 1 hour before serving, to chill. Makes 4 servings.

sweet-and-sour
cucumbers

4 medium-size cucumbers
2 teaspoons salt
½ cup half-and-half
2 tablespoons cider vinegar
2 tablespoons granulated sugar

Peel cucumbers. Using a potato peeler, slice cucumbers paper-thin. Sprinkle salt over cucumbers; squeeze with your hands to remove juice from cucumbers. After juice has formed, let cucumbers set in their own juice at room temperature 1 hour.

Add cream, vinegar, and sugar to cucumbers. Mix well. Chill. Makes 4 servings.

sour cucumbers
with bread

4 medium-size cucumbers
2 teaspoons salt
½ cup table cream
¼ cup cider vinegar
4 slices white bread
½ teaspoon black pepper, peppermill-ground

Peel cucumbers. Using a potato peeler, slice cucumbers paper-thin. Sprinkle salt over sliced cucumbers. Squeeze cucumbers with your hands to remove juice. After juice has formed, let cucumbers and juice stand at room temperature 1 hour to wilt cucumbers.

Add cream and vinegar to cucumbers. Mix well. Chill before serving.

Serve cucumbers over bread slices. Garnish with pepper. Makes 4 servings.

18

cucumbers in sour cream

4 cucumbers, garden-fresh
1 cup sour cream with chives
1 small bunch leaf lettuce, cleaned
1 tablespoon parsley

Wash cucumbers thoroughly; slice into small wedges.

Combine sour cream and cucumbers. Mix to coat cucumbers.

To serve, arrange lettuce leaves in salad bowls and pour ½ cup cucumber mixture on top of lettuce bed. Garnish with parsley before serving. Makes 4 servings.

cucumbers in sour cream

tongue and potato salad

2 cups diced cooked potatoes
1 small onion, chopped fine
2 cups diced cold cooked tongue
2 hard-cooked eggs, chopped
2 tablespoons chopped fresh parsley
¾ cup commercial Russian salad dressing
4 lettuce cups

Combine potatoes, onion, tongue, eggs, and parsley; toss gently to mix.

Pour salad dressing over potato mixture; mix well. Chill thoroughly.

To serve, arrange lettuce cups on salad plates and fill with tongue and potato salad. Makes 4 servings.

sauerkraut salad

4 cups drained sauerkraut
¼ cup minced onion
2 hard-cooked eggs, chopped
⅓ cup salad oil
2 tablespoons wine vinegar
⅓ cup sauerkraut juice
1 teaspoon dry mustard
2 teaspoons granulated sugar
¼ teaspoon white pepper

In salad bowl, combine sauerkraut, onion, and hard-cooked eggs. Mix.

Combine remaining ingredients in a jar; shake vigorously.

Add dressing mixture to kraut mixture; toss lightly. Makes 6 servings.

fresh garden salad

2 cucumbers
½ cup white vinegar
½ cup water
1 teaspoon salt
12 cherry tomatoes, sliced into circles
1 green pepper, sliced thin
1 small sweet onion, peeled and cut into rings
1 tablespoon chopped parsley for garnish

Peel cucumbers; slice them crosswise.

Combine vinegar, water, and salt. Pour over cucumbers; marinate at room temperature 2 hours. Drain. Add remaining vegetables to cucumbers; toss lightly. Chill before serving.

To serve, arrange on salad plates and garnish with parsley. Makes 4 servings.

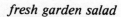

fresh garden salad

20

mushroom and sour-cream salad

2 cups canned mushroom slices, drained
½ cup wine vinegar
4 heads Boston lettuce
½ cup sour cream
1 tablespoon chopped fresh parsley

Combine mushroom slices and vinegar; marinate in refrigerator 24 hours. Drain.

Arrange lettuce on salad plate. Place ½ cup marinated mushrooms in center of lettuce bed; garnish with 2 tablespoons sour cream and fresh parsley. Makes 4 servings.

mushroom and sour-cream salad

sliced-mushroom salad

1 cup canned sliced mushrooms
¼ cup finely chopped onions
⅓ cup salad oil
¼ cup tarragon vinegar
4 heads Boston lettuce
¼ teaspoon black pepper, peppermill-ground

Drain liquid from mushrooms; pour into quart jar. Add onions, oil, and vinegar to mushrooms in quart jar. Cover; marinate for 24 hours, mixing occasionally.

Arrange lettuce heads on salad plates.

Drain mushrooms; arrange ¼ cup marinated mushrooms on each lettuce bed. Garnish with black pepper. Makes 4 servings.

cold polish potato salad

6 medium potatoes, cooked

marinade
¼ cup salad oil (olive oil may be used)
¼ cup cider vinegar
1 teaspoon dry mustard
1 teaspoon salt
½ teaspoon white pepper
1 tablespoon caraway seeds

1 medium onion, chopped fine
½ cup salad dressing
2 hard-cooked eggs, chopped
1 teaspoon paprika

Dice cooked potatoes into large bowl.

For marinade pour oil, vinegar, mustard, salt, white pepper, and caraway seeds into a jar. Seal jar; shake vigorously.

Pour marinade mixture over potatoes; marinate for 1 hour. Add onion, salad dressing, and chopped eggs. Toss just enough to mix.

Place potato salad in serving bowl and garnish with paprika. Makes 8 servings.

warsaw salad

2 medium-size cucumbers
6 large white radishes
2 Delicious apples
½ cup sour cream
2 tablespoons lemon juice
1 tablespoon finely chopped fresh parsley
1 teaspoon black pepper, peppermill-ground

Wash cucumbers and radishes thoroughly; slice them paper-thin. Combine.

Wash and core apples; slice into thin slices. Add to vegetables; toss to mix.

Combine sour cream and lemon juice.

To serve, place vegetable and fruit mixture in serving bowl; top with dressing. Garnish salad with chopped parsley and freshly ground black pepper. Makes 4 servings.

Picture on opposite page: warsaw salad

herring dinner salad

8 ounces salt-herring fillets
4 medium potatoes
1 cup chopped pickled beets
¼ cup chopped dill pickles
4-ounce can mushroom slices, drained
½ cup mayonnaise
¼ cup milk
¾ teaspoon salt
½ teaspoon white pepper
¼ teaspoon garlic powder
¼ teaspoon nutmeg
4 hard-cooked eggs
2 teaspoons mayonnaise
¼ teaspoon mixed Italian spices
2 sprigs parsley, chopped

Soak the herring filets in cold water overnight.

Boil potatoes in their jackets. Chill. Peel and cube potatoes.

Remove herring from water; dry thoroughly. Dice herring into bite-size pieces; add to potatoes. Add beets, pickles, and mushroom slices. Toss fish and vegetables to mix.

Mix ½ cup mayonnaise with milk. Add ½ teaspoon salt, ¼ teaspoon white pepper, garlic powder, and nutmeg. Beat until well-blended. Pour mayonnaise mixture over herring and vegetables; mix gently. Refrigerate for 1 hour.

Peel hard-cooked eggs; cut in half. Remove yolks from whites; force yolks through a sieve. Season yolks with 2 teaspoons mayonnaise, ¼ teaspoon salt (optional), and ¼ teaspoon white pepper. Mix well.

Fill egg-white halves with egg-yolk mixture; sprinkle with Italian seasonings.

Remove herring and vegetables from refrigerator; arrange filled eggs on top of salad. Garnish with parsley before serving. Makes 4 servings.

fresh raw-spinach salad

½ pound raw spinach
¼ cup chopped green pepper
½ Bermuda onion, cut into rings
1½ tablespoons lemon juice
1 tablespoon salad oil
½ teaspoon salt
¼ teaspoon black pepper, peppermill-ground
3 hard-cooked eggs
¼ cup anchovies

Thoroughly wash spinach, drain it, and wrap it in clean towel to dry. Tear spinach leaves into bite-size pieces; put into large salad bowl. Add green pepper, onion rings, lemon juice, salad oil, salt, and pepper. Toss lightly, just enough to mix.

To serve, garnish with hard-cooked eggs and anchovies. Makes 6 servings.

liverwurst salad

1 cup diced liverwurst
¼ cup finely chopped onion
¼ cup diced celery
¼ cup finely chopped green pepper
½ head lettuce, torn into medium-size pieces
½ cup shredded carrots

salad dressing
⅓ cup salad oil
⅓ cup salad vinegar
⅓ cup chili sauce
1 tablespoon prepared horseradish
½ teaspoon salt

Combine liverwurst, onion, celery, green pepper, lettuce, and carrots in salad bowl. Chill mixture thoroughly.

Combine dressing ingredients in a jar; shake vigorously. Chill.

To serve, place vegetable and meat mixture in salad bowls. Pour dressing mixture into a small pitcher and pass to guests. Makes 6 servings.

creamy fruit dressing

A colorful dressing for fruit salads.

1 cup creamed small-curd cottage cheese
½ cup sour cream
¼ teaspoon salt
½ cup maraschino cherry juice
1 tablespoon lemon juice

Force cottage cheese through a sieve; fold in sour cream. Add salt, cherry juice, and lemon juice; blend well. Chill before serving. Makes 1¾ cups.

cottage-cheese salad dressing

¼ cup lemon juice
¾ cup olive oil
1 teaspoon salt
¼ teaspoon white pepper
½ teaspoon dry mustard
2 tablespoons small-curd cottage cheese
1 tablespoon sweet pickle relish
1 tablespoon chopped parsley

Mix lemon juice, olive oil, salt, white pepper, and dry mustard in a glass jar; cover tightly, and shake until thoroughly blended. Add cottage cheese, pickle relish, and chopped parsley. Mix well. Chill before serving. Makes 1¼ cups.

vegetable dressing with cottage cheese

A unique dressing for green salads.

1 cup creamed cottage cheese
½ cup sour cream
¼ teaspoon onion salt
¼ teaspoon dry mustard
½ cup V-8 juice
2 tablespoons catsup
1 tablespoon steak sauce

Force cottage cheese through a sieve; fold in sour cream. Sprinkle onion salt and dry mustard over mixture; gently blend in. Add V-8 juice, catsup, and steak sauce; mix well. Chill thoroughly before serving. Makes 1¾ cups.

sour-cream salad dressing

3 egg yolks, hard-cooked
½ cup sour cream
¼ cup half-and-half
1 tablespoon vinegar
¼ teaspoon dillweed
½ teaspoon salt
¼ teaspoon black pepper
2 tablespoons chopped fresh parsley
3 egg whites, hard-cooked

Mash hard-cooked yolks until they resemble a fine meal. Stir in sour cream, half-and-half, and vinegar. Mix thoroughly. Add dillweed, salt, pepper, and parsley. Mix well.

Chop hard-cooked egg whites into fine pieces. Stir egg whites into cream mixture. Chill thoroughly before serving. Makes 1½ cups.

vegetables

honeyed carrot nuggets

2 10-ounce packages frozen carrot nuggets

honey butter
¼ cup butter
¼ cup honey

Cook carrot nuggets according to package directions. Drain.

Melt butter in shallow saucepan. Add honey to melted butter. Heat Honey Butter until bubbles start to form on surface.

Arrange carrots on serving platter; pour Honey Butter over carrots. Serve immediately. Makes 4 servings.

green beans in mushroom sauce

1 1-pound can cut green beans
1 can cream of mushroom soup
½ cup Dilled Croutons (see Index)

Combine green beans and soup. Mix well. Pour green-bean and soup mixture into greased 1-quart casserole dish. Top mixture with Dilled Croutons. Bake in preheated 350°F oven 20 minutes or until soup begins to bubble. Makes 4 servings.

Picture on next pages:
honeyed carrot nuggets
spiced green beans
cauliflower with buttered bread crumbs
paprika-buttered broccoli

marinated mushroom caps
seasoned peas
broiled tomatoes
steamed white asparagus

steamed white asparagus

2 pounds white asparagus
⅓ cup butter
⅔ cup water
1 teaspoon salt

Break off each asparagus stalk as far as it will snap off easily. Peel off scales with a potato peeler. Rinse several times to remove sand.

Heat butter and water to a boil in a pan large enough to accommodate asparagus stalks. Add asparagus and salt to boiling water; cover pan. Cook over high heat 12 minutes or until asparagus is fork-tender.

Drain; serve immediately. Makes 6 servings.

cauliflower with buttered bread crumbs

1 head cauliflower
1 teaspoon salt

buttered bread crumbs
¼ cup butter
3 tablespoons bread crumbs
¼ teaspoon white pepper

Wash cauliflower head; remove large outside leaves.

Select a saucepan large enough to accommodate the head of cauliflower. Cover bottom of pan with 1 to 2 inches of water. Add salt to water; bring water to rapid boil. Add cauliflower head to saucepan; cover. Boil cauliflower 25 minutes or until fork-tender. Drain immediately.

Brown butter in small skillet. Add bread crumbs and white pepper; stir until all butter is absorbed into the bread crumbs.

Place cooked cauliflower head on serving platter. Garnish with Buttered Bread Crumbs. Serve immediately. Makes 8 servings.

cauliflower ala poland

2 hard-cooked egg yolks
1 teaspoon dried parsley flakes
2 tablespoons sour cream
¼ teaspoon white pepper
1 head cauliflower
1 teaspoon salt
¼ cup butter
3 tablespoons bread crumbs

Mash egg yolks in a small bowl. Add parsley flakes, sour cream, and white pepper to egg yolks. Blend. Reserve for later.

Wash cauliflower head; remove outside leaves.

Select a saucepan large enough to accommodate the head of cauliflower. Cover bottom of pan with 1 to 2 inches of water. Add salt to water; bring water to rapid boil. Add cauliflower to saucepan; cover. Boil cauliflower 25 minutes or until fork-tender. Drain immediately.

Melt butter; stir in bread crumbs. Pour buttered bread crumbs over cauliflower; garnish with reserved egg-yolk mixture. Makes 8 servings.

cauliflower ala poland

spiced
green beans

The secret to using commercially canned vegetables is to remember the vegetables have been cooked in the canning process. Therefore, when serving canned vegetables, only reheat them.

2 1-pound cans whole green beans
¼ cup butter

lemon butter
2 tablespoons lemon juice
½ teaspoon salt
½ teaspoon dried basil
2 teaspoons dried parsley flakes

Drain green beans.

Bring drained liquid to a boil in saucepan large enough to hold green beans horizontally when re-added to liquid. When liquid comes to a boil, reduce heat to simmer; add green beans. Simmer beans 4 minutes or until heated. Do not boil. Drain beans. Reserve liquid for soup stock.

Prepare Lemon Butter. Melt butter. Stir in lemon juice, spices, and parsley flakes.

Arrange green beans on serving platter; coat with Lemon Butter. Serve immediately. Makes 6 servings

buttered fresh
snap green beans

1½ pounds snap green beans, freshly picked
1¼ quarts water
1 teaspoon salt
2 tablespoons butter, melted

Snap ends off beans; wash beans thoroughly. Drain; rinse several times to remove sand and grit.

Bring water to a rapid boil in large saucepan. Add salt and green beans to boiling water; boil for 20 minutes or until fork-tender. Drain.

Pour melted butter over green beans and arrange on serving platter. Serve immediately. Makes 6 servings.

sautéed
red cabbage

A traditional holiday meal in Warsaw.

2 tablespoons bacon fat
1 head red cabbage, shredded
1 large onion, sliced thin
1 tart cooking apple, cored and shredded
¼ cup cider vinegar
1 tablespoon granulated sugar
½ teaspoon salt
¼ teaspoon black pepper
Water as needed

Melt bacon fat in large skillet. Add remaining ingredients to skillet. Stir to mix. Cover skillet; simmer vegetables 1 hour or until tender. Add water as needed to prevent sticking. Makes 8 servings.

paprika-buttered broccoli

1 cup water
1 teaspoon salt
2 10-ounce packages frozen whole broccoli

paprika butter
¼ cup butter
½ teaspoon salt
¼ teaspoon white pepper
¼ teaspoon paprika

Bring water to rapid boil in saucepan. Add 1 teaspoon salt and broccoli; continue to boil for 15 minutes or until broccoli is fork-tender but not mushy. Drain immediately.

Make Paprika Butter by melting butter; stir in ½ teaspoon salt, white pepper, and paprika.

Arrange broccoli on serving platter. Pour Paprika Butter over broccoli. Serve immediately. Makes 6 servings.

marinated mushroom caps

2 cups canned mushroom caps

marinade
½ cup finely chopped onions
½ cup salad vinegar
½ teaspoon black pepper, peppermill-ground
½ teaspoon garlic powder
½ cup salad oil

Drain mushrooms; pour into quart jar.

Combine Marinade ingredients. Add Marinade to jar and marinate mushrooms for 24 hours, mixing 3 or 4 times during marinating period.

To serve, drain mushrooms and arrange on serving platter. Makes 6 servings.

brussels sprouts with parmesan cheese

1½ pounds Brussels sprouts
1 cup water
1 teaspoon salt
¼ teaspoon white pepper
¼ cup butter, melted
¼ cup Parmesan cheese

Clean Brussels sprouts, being sure to remove all tough and bruised outer leaves. Cover Brussels sprouts with cold water; soak for 30 minutes. Drain.

In saucepan large enough to accommodate Brussels sprouts, bring 1 cup water to a rapid boil. Add salt and Brussels sprouts to boiling water; cover. Continue to cook Brussels sprouts 15 minutes or until fork-tender. Drain.

Combine pepper and butter; pour over Brussels sprouts. Garnish with Parmesan cheese. Makes 4 servings.

french-fried eggplant

1 medium eggplant
1 cup all-purpose white flour
½ teaspoon salt
¼ teaspoon black pepper
1 egg, beaten
½ cup milk
1 cup bread crumbs

Peel eggplant; cut into ¾-inch strips. Combine flour and spices in a shallow bowl.

Combine egg and milk in another shallow bowl.

Pour bread crumbs into a third shallow bowl.

Dip eggplant strips in seasoned flour, then in egg mixture; shake, then dip into crumbs and shake again.

Fry breaded strips in oil heated to 375°F for 4 minutes, turning them once during cooking period. Drain on a brown paper bag. Makes 4 servings.

seasoned parsnips

1½ pounds parsnips
Small piece salt pork
¼ cup butter, melted

Wash, peel, and core parsnips. Cut into strips; add to boiling salted water, along with salt pork. Boil parsnips 25 minutes or until fork-tender. Drain.

Serve coated with melted butter. Makes 4 servings.

seasoned peas

2 pounds fresh peas, shelled
2 cups water
1 teaspoon salt

dilled butter
¼ cup butter
½ teaspoon white pepper
2 tablespoons chopped fresh dill

Wash peas thoroughly in cold water. Drain.

Bring water to rapid boil in large saucepan. Add peas and salt. Cover pan; continue to cook for 15 minutes or until peas are tender. Drain.

Melt butter in a small saucepan. Stir in pepper and chopped dill.

Pour peas in serving dish and cover with Dilled Butter. Makes 6 servings.

33

broiled tomatoes

4 medium tomatoes

seasoned butter
¼ cup butter
1 teaspoon garlic salt
¼ teaspoon white pepper
¼ teaspoon dry mustard

Wash tomatoes. Place upside down on broiler pan. With a sharp knife, slash skins of tomatoes in an "X" design.

Make Seasoned Butter. Melt butter; stir in garlic salt, white pepper, and dry mustard.

Brush tomatoes with Seasoned Butter.

Place broiling pan in farthest slot from flame. Broil tomatoes 2 minutes. Remove tomatoes from broiler; baste tomatoes again with Seasoned Butter. Return tomatoes to broiler; continue to broil for an additional 3 minutes. Makes 4 servings.

dilled tomato cups with peas

4 medium tomatoes

seasoned butter
2 tablespoons butter, melted
½ teaspoon salt
¼ teaspoon white pepper
½ teaspoon dried dillweed

½ cup water
1 cup peas, frozen

Slice tops from tomatoes; spoon out centers, being sure not to damage the structure of the tomato walls.

Melt butter. Add salt, white pepper, and dillweed.

Brush insides of tomatoes with Seasoned Butter. Bake tomatoes in 400°F oven 15 minutes or until tender.

While tomatoes are baking, bring ½ cup water to rapid boil. Add peas; cook for 8 to 10 minutes or until tender.

To serve, fill tomato halves with hot peas. Serve immediately. Makes 4 servings.

parsley buttered potatoes

1 to 1½ pounds new potatoes
1 cup water
1 teaspoon salt
⅓ cup butter, melted
1 tablespoon dried parsley flakes

With a paring knife, scrape skins from new potatoes*.

Bring water and salt to a rolling boil. Add potatoes, cover, and simmer for 20 minutes or until fork-tender. Drain.

Pour potatoes into serving bowl, coat with melted butter, and sprinkle with parsley flakes. Makes 4 servings.

*Do not use a potato peeler. The skins of new potatoes are too thin to remove them with a potato peeler.

stuffed baked tomatoes

stuffed baked tomatoes

4 large tomatoes
¼ cup butter
½ cup finely chopped onions
½ cup tomato centers (from above tomatoes)
½ teaspoon salt
¼ teaspoon black pepper
¼ teaspoon oregano
2 cups bread crumbs
1 bunch parsley

Thoroughly wash tomatoes. Dry on a paper towel. With a sharp knife, remove tops from tomatoes. Save tomato tops for later use. Scoop centers from tomatoes; reserve ½ cup for later use.

Heat butter in medium-size skillet. Add onions; cook until tender. Add ½ cup tomato centers to onions; cook until tomato pieces are mushy.

Combine spices and bread crumbs. Add cooked vegetables and butter. Work bread and vegetables with your hands until well-combined and stuffing mix has formed. If stuffing mix is too dry, add more melted butter.

Fill tomato cavities with stuffing mixture. Place tomatoes close together in a slightly greased baking pan. If tomatoes are small enough, they can be baked in a greased muffin tin. Replace tomato tops. Bake tomatoes in 350°F oven 30 minutes or until fork-tender.

Carefully arrange tomatoes on serving platter. Garnish with fresh parsley. Makes 4 servings.

35

creamed peas and corn

parsley buttered potatoes

creamed peas and corn

1 10-ounce package frozen peas
1 10-ounce package frozen corn

white sauce
2 tablespoons butter
2 tablespoons all-purpose white flour
1 cup milk
½ teaspoon salt
¼ teaspoon white pepper

Cook peas and corn as directed on packages.

While vegetables are cooking, make White Sauce. Melt butter in saucepan; add flour. Cook for 2 minutes, stirring constantly. Add milk, salt, and pepper; stir and continue to cook until White Sauce forms. Remove from heat.

Drain cooked vegetables. Add White Sauce to vegetables. Mix well. Serve immediately. Makes 6 servings.

polish chicory

Delicious served with roast veal and potatoes.

6 chicory heads
1½ cups water
1 teaspoon salt
1 teaspoon white vinegar
¼ teaspoon white pepper
8 tablespoons butter
2 hard-cooked eggs
1 bunch parsley

Clean and wash chicory; cut out the bitter center.

Bring water, salt, white vinegar, white pepper, and 2 tablespoons butter to a boil. Reduce liquid to simmer; add chicory. Simmer for 15 minutes. Drain.

Brown remaining 6 tablespoons butter; pour over cooked chicory.

Chop eggs and parsley. Chop and garnish chicory. Makes 6 servings.

polish chicory

potatoes with bacon

2 pounds small round potatoes
1 teaspoon salt
4 strips bacon

Peel potatoes, wash well, and cover with water. Add salt to water; bring to a boil. Reduce heat to simmer; cook, covered, for 25 minutes or until done. Drain; cut into bite-size pieces.

Cut bacon into small pieces; fry until brown and crisp.

To serve, pour bacon and bacon drippings over cooked potatoes. Makes 4 servings.

potatoes with bacon

fried potatoes with sausage

38

hot bacon
potato salad

The secret of this potato salad is the addition of freshly cooked potatoes rather than cold sliced potatoes.

4 medium potatoes
2 slices bacon
½ cup chopped onions
¼ cup finely chopped celery
1 tablespoon flour
½ cup water
¼ cup wine vinegar
½ teaspoon salt
¼ teaspoon black pepper
1 tablespoon honey
¼ teaspoon dried dillweed

In a large saucepan cover potatoes with cold water; bring to rapid boil. Reduce heat; continue cooking for 20 minutes or until potatoes can be punctured easily with a dinner fork. Drain. Peel potatoes and slice into small pieces.

While potatoes are cooking, fry bacon in a large skillet until crisp. Remove bacon from skillet; drain on a paper towel to remove excess grease.

Sauté chopped onions and celery in hot bacon grease until wilted. Stir in flour; stir to blend. Add water and vinegar; stir and cook until liquid is thickened. Add salt, pepper, honey, dillweed, and potatoes. Stir just enough to mix, being careful not to mash potatoes.

Crumble cooked bacon and use it to garnish potato salad just before serving. Makes 4 servings.

fried potatoes
with sausage

A delicious midnight snack served with beer and rye bread.

1 pound Kielbasa
4 large white potatoes, peeled and sliced
1 tablespoon chopped fresh parsley

Slice Kielbasa; fry in large skillet. Remove Kielbasa from skillet.

Add potatoes to skillet. Fry on one side without stirring. When done on one side, use a pancake turner and flip potatoes with one turn. Fry remaining side of potatoes until done.

To serve, garnish with fried Kielbasa and parsley. Makes 4 servings.

39

creamed corn

A great use for leftover corn on the cob.

4 large ears corn

cream sauce
1 tablespoon butter
1 tablespoon all-purpose white flour
1 cup half-and-half
½ teaspoon salt
¼ teaspoon white pepper

Place corn in large saucepan; cover with cold water. Bring water to a boil. Reduce heat to simmer; continue cooking corn 10 minutes. Drain. When corn ears are cool enough to handle, remove kernels from husks, being careful not to cut into husks.

Prepare Cream Sauce. Make a roux by melting the butter in a 2-quart saucepan. Stir in flour, making sure flour and butter are well-blended. Gradually add half-and-half to the roux, stirring constantly to prevent lumping. Continue cooking sauce until it has thickened. Add salt and pepper. Mix well.

Stir corn kernels into Cream Sauce. Serve immediately. Makes 4 servings.

breads, dumplings, and noodles

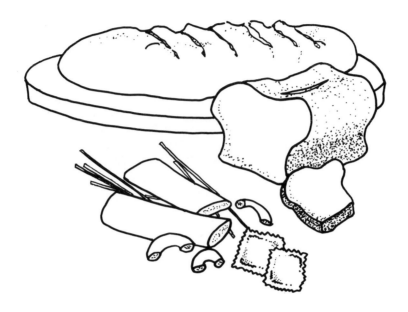

onion biscuits

2 cups all-purpose white flour
2½ teaspoons baking powder
1 teaspoon salt
⅓ cup shortening
¾ cup milk
¼ cup grated onions
2 tablespoons butter, melted
1 tablespoon poppy seeds

Heat oven to 450°F.

Combine dry ingredients; cut in shortening to resemble cornmeal. Add milk and grated onions; stir just enough to mix.

Turn dough out onto a floured surface; knead lightly. Roll dough out to ½ inch thick. Cut close together with floured biscuit cutter. Place biscuits on ungreased cookie sheet.

Brush biscuit tops with melted butter; sprinkle with poppy seeds. Bake in 450°F oven 10 to 12 minutes or until golden brown. Makes 20 biscuits.

nut rolls

1 package active dry yeast
¼ cup lukewarm water
¾ cup milk
½ cup butter
1 cup granulated sugar
1 teaspoon salt

2 eggs, beaten
4 to 5 cups all-purpose white flour
½ cup brown sugar
1 tablespoon cinnamon
¼ cup butter, melted
1 cup chopped English walnuts

Dissolve yeast in warm water.

Scald milk. Add ½ cup butter, ½ cup sugar, and salt; stir until shortening dissolves. Cool milk mixture to lukewarm; pour into dissolved yeast mixture. Mix well. Add beaten eggs and flour. Stir until flour is worked in and a dough has formed.

Turn dough out onto floured surface; knead for 10 minutes or until a smooth dough has formed. Place dough in greased bowl. Cover; let rise until doubled in bulk, about 1 hour. Punch down.

Combine ½ cup granulated sugar, brown sugar, and cinnamon.

Divide dough into 2 equal parts. On floured surface roll dough into 2 oblongs measuring 8 × 16 inches. Spread each oblong with equal parts of ¼ cup melted butter. Over the butter, sprinkle the sugar and cinnamon mixture evenly between the 2 dough oblongs. Finally, sprinkle ½ cup English walnuts on top of dough oblongs. Roll dough jelly-roll fashion, being sure to seal edges to prevent leakage. Cut each oblong into 16 equal pieces. Place in greased muffin tins. Cover; let rise until double in bulk, about 45 minutes.

Bake in preheated 350°F oven 25 minutes or until golden brown. Remove from muffin tins; cool.

Nut rolls may be glazed while still warm (see Index). Makes 32 rolls.

poppy-seed egg roll

2 packages active dry yeast
1 cup lukewarm water
1 teaspoon granulated sugar
½ cup milk
½ cup half-and-half
2½ teaspoons salt

⅓ cup sugar
2 eggs, beaten
6½ to 7 cups all-purpose white flour
⅓ cup butter, melted
4 12-ounce cans poppy-seed filling
½ cup butter, melted

Soften yeast in lukewarm water with 1 teaspoon sugar.

Combine milk and half-and-half; scald. Stir in salt and ⅓ cup sugar; cool to lukewarm. Stir in yeast mixture. Add beaten eggs; mix well. Stir in 4 cups flour; beat until smooth. Add ⅓ cup melted butter; beat until mixed. Knead in enough remaining dough to form a medium-soft dough. Knead dough 10 minutes or until smooth and elastic. Place in lightly greased bowl; grease top. Cover; let rise in warm place until doubled in bulk.

Punch down and divide dough in half. Roll each dough half into a 12 × 18-inch rectangle. Spread 2 cans poppy-seed filling over each piece of dough. Starting at one end, roll dough jelly-roll fashion halfway. Repeat process, starting at other end. Prepare remaining dough in same manner. Place rolls on greased cookie sheets. Cover; let rise until doubled in bulk.

Brush tops with melted butter; bake in 400°F oven 30 minutes or until golden brown.

Glaze (see Index) while still warm. Makes 2 rolls.

Picture on opposite page: poppy-seed egg roll

poppy-seed kuchen

½ cup milk
½ cup half-and-half
¾ cup butter
1 cup granulated sugar
1 teaspoon salt
1 package active dry yeast
2 eggs, beaten

4 to 5 cups all-purpose white flour
1 cup raisins
½ cup water
¼ cup vodka
1 can poppy-seed filling
1 cup chopped English walnuts
⅔ cup all-purpose flour

Combine milk and half-and-half; scald them. Add ½ cup butter, ½ cup sugar, and salt to scalded-milk mixture; stir until butter dissolves. Cool to lukewarm. Add yeast; mix well. Add eggs and 4 cups flour. Stir until flour is worked in and a dough forms.

Turn dough onto floured surface; work in enough remaining flour to form medium-stiff dough. Knead dough for 10 minutes or until a smooth dough forms. Place dough in greased bowl; cover and let rise until doubled in bulk, about 1 hour.

While dough is rising, combine raisins, water, and vodka in small saucepan. Simmer until raisins absorb all liquid.

Combine poppy-seed filling, nuts, and raisins. Mix well.

Punch down dough; divide it into 2 equal parts. Roll each dough ball into a 12 × 10-inch rectangle. Spread filling evenly over rectangles.

Combine ¼ cup butter, ¼ cup sugar, and flour; mix well. Spread over poppy-seed filling. Cover; let kuchen rise until doubled in bulk.

Bake in 350°F oven 30 minutes or until dough is golden brown. Makes 2 kuchen.

poppy-seed kuchen

kielbasa and cheese loaf

¾ cup warm water
1 package hot-roll mix
1 egg, beaten
½ cup grated Swiss cheese
½ cup cooked, finely chopped Kielbasa
¼ cup butter, melted

Pour ¾ cup warm water into a medium-size bowl. Sprinkle yeast from roll mix over the water; stir until dissolved. Add beaten egg; mix well. Blend in flour from roll mix, Swiss cheese, and Kielbasa. Continue blending until all ingredients are combined to form a sticky dough ball. Cover; let dough rise in a warm place until doubled in bulk, about 45 minutes. Punch down.

Work dough on floured surface to form an oblong roll. Place loaf on greased baking sheet. Cover loosely. Let bread rise again in warm place until light and doubled in size, about 30 minutes.

Brush top of loaf with melted butter. Bake in preheated 400°F oven 30 minutes or until bread is golden brown. Remove loaf from oven; cool it on a rack. Makes 1 loaf.

kielbasa and cheese loaf

dumplings

1½ cups all-purpose white flour
2 egg yolks
¾ cup beef broth
1 teaspoon salt
¼ teaspoon white pepper
1 quart beef bouillon

Mix flour, egg yolks, beef broth, salt, and white pepper. Beat vigorously. If batter is too thin, add additional flour.

Using a teaspoon, drop batter into boiling bouillon. When dumplings float to top, soup is ready to serve. Makes 4 servings.

dumplings

stew dumplings

1 cup mashed potatoes
2 teaspoons shortening
¼ cup bread crumbs
2 tablespoons flour
¼ teaspoon paprika
¼ teaspoon celery seed
¼ teaspoon dried minced parsley
1 egg yolk
½ bunch fresh parsley

Mix ingredients thoroughly.

Dust your hands generously with flour. Shape potato dough into 2-inch balls by rolling dough between the palms of your hands. Ten minutes before serving time, place dumplings on top of cooking stew. Cover and steam for 10 minutes.

Remove dumplings from stew and arrange on serving platter. Garnish with parsley. Makes 4 servings.

buttered noodles

Garnished with catsup, noodles make a delicious substitute for potatoes.

4 cups water
½ teaspoon salt
2 cups medium-size noodles
¼ cup butter, melted

Bring water to a boil in large saucepan. Add salt and noodles. Stir with a fork to prevent sticking. Adjust heat; boil noodles for 15 minutes or until fork-tender. Drain.

Pour noodles into serving dish and coat with butter. Serve immediately. Makes 4 servings.

homemade noodles

Delicious with homemade chicken soup.

2¾ cups all-purpose white flour
2 eggs, lightly beaten
¼ cup cold water*
½ cup butter, melted

Combine 2½ cups flour and eggs; mix well. Add cold water 1 tablespoon at a time until a stiff dough forms. Work dough until bubbles begin to form. Roll dough out to about ⅛ inch thick; sprinkle with remaining flour. Let dough stand until dry. Cut into strips; drop into boiling salted water. Cook for 20 minutes. Stir while cooking to prevent sticking.

Drain noodles and serve with melted butter. Makes 6 servings.

*The amount of water needed will vary with the brand of flour used and the humidity in the air.

47

round potato bread

1 cup milk
¼ cup margarine
⅓ cup granulated sugar
1 cup mashed potatoes, unseasoned
6 cups all-purpose white flour
2 eggs, beaten
2 packages active dry yeast
½ cup lukewarm water
1 teaspoon salt
2 tablespoons all-purpose white flour

Scald milk; add margarine, sugar, and mashed potatoes. Cool to lukewarm. Add 1 cup flour; stir in. Add eggs; mix well.

Dissolve yeast in lukewarm water. Add to above mixture; mix well. Cover; let rest until mixture bubbles, about 1½ hours. Stir down. Add enough remaining flour to form a stiff dough.

Turn dough out onto floured surface; knead until dough is smooth and elastic, about 10 minutes. Place in greased bowl. Cover; let rise until doubled in bulk. Punch down; form into 2 round loaves. Cover; let rise until loaves double in size.

With a sharp knife make an "X" design on the top of each loaf. Dust the top of each loaf with 1 tablespoon flour. Bake in 375°F oven 40 minutes or until loaves are evenly browned. Makes 2 loaves.

brown-and-serve dinner rolls

1 cup milk
½ cup all-vegetable shortening
⅓ cup granulated sugar
1 teaspoon salt
1 package active dry yeast
2 eggs, beaten
4 to 5 cups unbleached white flour

Scald milk; add shortening, sugar, and salt. Stir until shortening dissolves. Cool to lukewarm. Add yeast; mix well. Add eggs and flour. Stir until flour is worked in and a dough forms.

Turn dough out onto floured surface; knead for 10 minutes or until a smooth dough forms. Place dough in a greased bowl. Cover bowl; let dough rise until doubled in bulk, about 1 hour. Punch down. Shape into rolls. Cover; let rise until doubled in bulk.

Bake rolls at 257°F until slightly brown, about 12 to 15 minutes. Remove from baking tray; seal in freezing bags. Freeze immediately.

To serve rolls, remove from freezing bags and bake at 450°F for 10 minutes. Serve immediately. Makes 2 dozen.

orange bread sticks

¼ cup milk
¼ cup granulated sugar
½ teaspoon salt
2¼ cups all-purpose flour
¼ cup butter
1 package active dry yeast
¼ cup warm water
1 egg, beaten
½ cup chopped English walnuts
1 tablespoon grated orange peel
½ cup candied fruit
¼ cup white raisins
¼ cup granulated sugar

Scald milk. Cool to lukewarm.

Combine sugar, salt, and flour. Cut in butter.

Dissolve yeast in warm water. Stir in lukewarm milk. Add beaten egg and flour mixture; mix well. Place in greased bowl; grease top. Cover; let rise in warm place until doubled in bulk, about 1½ hours.

While dough is rising, combine remaining ingredients.

When dough has doubled in bulk, punch down and turn out on lightly floured board. Divide in half. Roll out each half into an oblong about 16 × 12 inches. Place one oblong on large greased baking sheet. Spread with nut and fruit mixture. Cover with remaining oblong of dough. Cover. Let rise in warm place until doubled in bulk, about 1 hour.

Bake sticks in 350°F oven 20 minutes or until golden brown. Cool.

Frost sticks with Orange Glaze. Cut into bars. Makes 20 bars.

orange glaze

1 cup confectioners' sugar
1 tablespoon orange juice
¼ teaspoon vanilla

Combine all ingredients. Mix well.

glaze for sweet breads

2 cups confectioners' sugar
2 to 3 tablespoons sour cream
1 teaspoon vanilla

Combine confectioners' sugar and liquid. Beat vigorously until glaze forms. Makes 2 cups.

49

pierogi

Pierogis are a favorite dish of Poland. They are served as a main dish with butter, as a dessert with sour cream, or are French-fried and garnished with mustard.

The dough used for all three types of Pierogis is the same. The fillings and garnishes vary the Pierogi dishes.

pierogi dough

2 cups all-purpose white flour
1 large egg or 2 small eggs
½ teaspoon salt
⅓ to ½ cup water

Mix flour, eggs, and salt. Stir in water until a stiff dough forms. Divide dough in half; roll paper-thin. Cut circles in dough with biscuit cutter. Place a teaspoon of filling on half the biscuit circle. Moisten edges. Fold over the unfilled side; seal edges. Drop into boiling salted water; cook for 3 to 5 minutes.

Using a slotted spoon, lift gently out of water and place in single layer on serving dish. Do not stack. Serve immediately. Makes dough for 4 to 6 servings.

cottage-cheese pierogis

1 cup dry cottage cheese
1 egg, beaten
½ teaspoon salt
¼ teaspoon black pepper, peppermill-ground
1 tablespoon chopped chives

Mix all ingredients together thoroughly.

Fill and cook Pierogis as instructed in directions given with Pierogi Dough recipe.

Serve Pierogis with melted butter. Makes 4 servings.

dessert pierogis

Prepare Pierogi Dough as directed. Fill dough circles with one of the following fillings:

1 cup pureed peach preserves
2 cups pitted fresh cherries
1 can apricot filling

To cook, drop into boiling salted water and cook for 3 to 5 minutes; or deep-fat fry in oil heated to 360°F until golden brown.

Serve Pierogis with sour cream. Makes 4 servings.

50

french-fried pierogis

1 cup mashed potatoes
½ cup grated cheddar cheese
1 egg, beaten
½ teaspoon salt
¼ teaspoon black pepper, peppermill-ground
Mustard

Combine all ingredients except mustard; mix well.

Prepare dough and fill Pierogis as instructed in directions given with Pierogi Dough recipe. Drop into frying oil preheated to 360°F. Fry until dough turns a golden brown.

To serve, garnish with mustard. Makes 4 servings.

hamburger and sauerkraut pierogis

½ pound hamburger
¼ cup minced onions
½ cup sauerkraut
Melted butter

Brown hamburger in skillet. Add onion; cook for 5 minutes. Drain fat; add sauerkraut. Mix well.

Fill and cook Pierogis as instructed in directions given in Pierogi Dough recipe.

Serve Pierogis with melted butter. Makes 4 servings.

caraway-seed-cheese rolls

Delicious served warm.

¾ cup warm water
1 package hot-roll mix
1 egg, beaten
½ cup shredded caraway-seed cheese
¼ cup butter, melted

Pour ¾ cup warm water into medium-size bowl. Sprinkle yeast from roll mix over water; stir until dissolved. Add beaten egg; mix well. Blend in flour from roll mix and caraway-seed cheese. Continue blending until all ingredients are combined to form a sticky dough. Let dough rise in warm place until doubled in bulk, about 45 minutes. Punch down.

Divide dough into 16 equal parts; shape into balls. Place in greased 13 × 9-inch pan. Cover. Let rise until doubled in bulk, about 45 minutes.

Brush ball tops with melted butter. Bake in preheated 400°F oven 15 minutes or until golden brown. Makes 16 rolls.

main dishes

fillet mignon in wine

4 2-inch-thick fillets mignons
1 teaspoon salt
½ teaspoon black pepper, peppermill-ground
¼ cup butter
4 small onions, peeled and halved
1 cup red wine

Rub fillets mignons with salt and pepper.

Melt butter in heavy frying pan. Add steaks to melted butter; brown on both sides. Reduce heat to simmer; add onion halves and wine. Cover skillet tightly; simmer steaks for 30 minutes. Makes 4 servings.

tomato and horseradish sauce

1 cup tomato catsup
2 tablespoons prepared horseradish

Combine catsup and horseradish. Mix thoroughly. Chill before serving. Makes 1 cup.

Picture on previous pages: fillet mignon in wine

david's liver patties

1 pound calves' liver
4 slices bacon
1 large onion
1 slice white bread
2 tablespoons bacon fat

Grind liver, bacon, and onion alternately in a food grinder. Grind bread after meat and onion have been ground, to clean out grinder. Mix thoroughly. Pour liver mixture into loaf pan; chill for 24 hours. Unmold liver loaf and slice into ½-inch pieces.

Heat bacon fat in frying pan. Fry liver slices until browned on both sides and cooked through.

Serve with Tomato-Horseradish Sauce (see Index). Makes 8 servings.

short ribs and cabbage

3 tablespoons shortening
4 pounds short ribs, cut into serving pieces
1 tablespoon salt
½ teaspoon black pepper
½ cup wine vinegar
1 cup water
½ teaspoon oregano
½ teaspoon dried horseradish
2 teaspoons dry mustard
1 bay leaf
½ cup onions, sliced crosswise
1 small head of cabbage, wedged

Melt shortening in large Dutch oven. Brown short ribs on all sides in melted shortening. Sprinkle with salt and pepper. Add remaining ingredients (except cabbage wedges). Cover Dutch oven; simmer 1 to 1½ hours. Add cabbage wedges; cook about 20 minutes, or until cabbage is tender. Makes 4 servings.

calf's liver in beer

¼ cup salad oil
1 large onion, cut into rings
1 pound calf's liver, cut into 1-inch pieces
3 tablespoons flour
1 cup stale beer
½ cup beef broth
1 teaspoon salt
½ teaspoon black pepper, peppermill-ground
1 cup sour cream

Heat oil in large skillet. Sauté onion rings until glassy and tender. Remove onion from oil. Add liver pieces to oil. Cook liver until brown and heated thoroughly, about 15 minutes. Remove liver from oil. Drain.

Measure oil remaining in skillet. If oil does not measure 3 tablespoons, add additional oil. Return oil to skillet; reheat. Add flour. Stir flour and oil to make a paste. Cook paste until golden brown. Add beer and beef broth to paste. Turn heat to high. Stir liquid and paste constantly to form gravy. Add spices. Stir in sour cream. Reheat. Fold liver and onions into gravy.

Serve liver with Buttered Noodles (see Index). Makes 4 servings.

chicken in dill sauce

2 chicken fryers, cut in pieces
1½ quarts boiling water
1 onion, quartered
2 celery stalks with leaves, chopped
3 peppercorns
5 tablespoons flour
⅓ cup cold water
1 teaspoon salt
2 tablespoons finely chopped fresh dill
½ cup sour cream

Cover chicken with boiling water; add onion, celery, and peppercorns. Cover; simmer for 2½ hours or until meat is fork-tender. Remove chicken from stock; keep it warm.

Strain stock; measure out 2¼ cups. Reheat the 2¼ cups stock.

Form a paste with flour and water. Slowly stir flour paste into heated stock; stir until stock thickens. Add salt, dill, and sour cream to thickened stock; stir to blend.

To serve, pour sauce over chicken pieces. Makes 6 servings.

chicken breasts with mushrooms

⅓ cup oil
4 chicken breasts with ribs
2 teaspoons salt
½ teaspoon black pepper
1 cup sliced fresh mushrooms
1 small can evaporated milk
1 small onion, sliced thin
4 white potatoes, sliced crosswise
1 sprig parsley

Heat oil in large skillet. Brown chicken breasts in oil until skin is golden brown. Transfer to glass baking dish. Sprinkle chicken with 1 teaspoon salt and ¼ teaspoon pepper.

Sauté mushrooms in oil used for browning chicken. Using a slotted spoon, drain oil from mushrooms back into skillet. Sprinkle mushrooms over browned chicken.

Cover chicken and cook in microwave oven on high for 10 minutes. Remove from oven; pour evaporated milk over mushrooms and chicken breasts. Return to microwave oven; cook on simmer 10 more minutes.*

While chicken breasts are cooking, sauté onion slices in oil used to brown chicken. When onion is clear, add potato slices; fry until tender. Sprinkle with 1 teaspoon salt and ¼ teaspoon pepper.

Arrange chicken and vegetables on serving tray. Garnish with parsley if desired. Makes 4 servings.

*In conventional oven, bake chicken covered 30 minutes at 325°F. Remove from oven; pour evaporated milk over chicken. Return to oven; bake for an additional 30 minutes.

scrambled eggs and sausage

½ pound pork sausage
8 eggs
¼ cup milk
1 teaspoon salt
¼ teaspoon black pepper, peppermill-ground

Sauté sausage in skillet until cooked and brown. Drain off fat.

Beat eggs, milk, salt, and pepper together. Pour egg mixture over sausage; stir until eggs are cooked. Makes 6 servings.

scrambled eggs with green-onion tops

½ cup green-onion tops
¼ cup oil
8 eggs
1 teaspoon salt
½ teaspoon black pepper

Remove green tops from spring onions; cut into small pieces. Save onions for use in a salad at a later meal.

Heat oil in skillet. Add chopped onion tops to heated oil; cook until glassy and slightly brown.

Whip eggs, salt, and pepper. Pour egg mixture into fried green-onion tops, stirring constantly to thoroughly mix eggs and onion tops. Continue stirring until eggs are scrambled.

Serve eggs immediately. Makes 4 servings.

roast guinea hen

2 2- to 3-pound dressed guinea hens
1½ teaspoons salt
1 lemon, quartered
2 small onions
4 slices country-style bacon, sliced
2 cups Dilled Croutons (see Index)
Tomato Cups with Peas (see Index)

Rub guinea hens inside and out with salt and lemon wedges. Insert an onion in each hen. Place bacon over back of hen. Roast in 325°F oven 40 minutes. Turn hens over in roasting pan; rearrange bacon over breasts of hens. Continue cooking for 35 to 40 minutes or until hen is fork-tender.

Place bird on a hot platter and garnish with Dilled Croutons and Tomato Cups with Peas. Makes 4 servings.

broiled sirloin
with mushrooms

4 1-inch-thick sirloin steaks
½ clove garlic
1 teaspoon salt
½ teaspoon black pepper, peppermill-ground
½ cup butter
2 cups sliced mushrooms

Rub steaks with garlic and sprinkle with half the salt and pepper. Score fatty edges of steak. Place meat on broiling pan 3 inches from heat. Broil on one side to desired degree of doneness. Turn meat; season uncooked side with remaining salt and pepper. Return meat to broiler; cook to desired doneness.

While steak is broiling, melt butter. Add mushrooms; sauté until golden brown and tender.

To serve, arrange steaks on serving platter and cover with sautéed mushrooms. Makes 4 servings.

mushroom-stuffed
onions

The peasants of Poland, who live primarily from the fruits of their labor, serve stuffed vegetables as the main course for the dinner meal.

4 large Spanish onions
Boiling water
2 hard rolls
¾ cup whole milk
2 tablespoons butter, melted
1 cup sliced fresh mushrooms
2 tablespoons water
½ teaspoon salt
¼ teaspoon black pepper
¼ cup butter
½ cup boiling water

Skin onions; place in large saucepan. Cover with boiling water. Boil for 15 minutes or until onion meat becomes wilted.

While onions are boiling, soak hard rolls in ¾ cup milk.

Melt butter in small skillet. Add mushrooms and 2 tablespoons water to butter. Stir to mix. Cover skillet; steam until mushrooms are limp. Stir occasionally to prevent mushrooms from sticking.

Form a stuffing base by squeezing soaked hard rolls until a bread and milk sponge develops. Add cooked mushrooms, salt, and pepper to bread sponge to form stuffing. Mix well.

Press out centers of onions; fill with stuffing mixture. Bake in 400°F oven 20 minutes or until tender.

Melt ¼ cup butter in ½ cup boiling water. Use this butter and water mixture to baste onions while they are baking. Makes 4 servings.

Picture on opposite page: broiled sirloin with mushrooms

hunter's stew

hunter's stew

3 pounds stewing-beef cubes	5 large carrots
1 quart water	2 sprigs parsley
8 peppercorns	4 celery stalks
8 whole cloves	3 leeks
2 whole bay leaves	½ cup butter
2 teaspoons salt	½ teaspoon white pepper
1 teaspoon marjoram	3 sprigs dill
3 pounds chicken, cubed	½ bunch parsley
2 medium onions	

Cover beef cubes with 1 quart water; bring to a boil.

Tie peppercorns, cloves, and bay leaves in a cloth bag; drop into boiling beef. Sprinkle 1 teaspoon salt and marjoram over beef; continue to simmer 2 hours in covered kettle. Add chicken cubes; continue to simmer, covered.

Peel onions and carrots; cut in rings.

Chop 2 sprigs parsley, celery, and leeks.

Put butter into a pan; add vegetables, 1 teaspoon salt, and pepper. Sauté vegetables over low heat until wilted.

Chop dill and remaining parsley.

Take cloth bag out of meat; discard. Remove meat from water.

Add wilted vegetables to meat stock; simmer until tender. Add meat back to stock and vegetables.

To serve, pour into serving dish and sprinkle with chopped dill and parsley. Makes 8 servings.

poached fillet of fish in shrimp sauce

poached fillet of fish in shrimp sauce

shrimp sauce

1 pound shrimp, cooked
⅓ cup butter
⅓ cup all-purpose white flour
1½ quarts half-and-half

1½ teaspoons paprika
3 teaspoons salt
½ teaspoon white pepper
1 cup canned mushroom caps

8 large white fish fillets
½ cup milk
½ cup water
2 sprigs parsley

Peel and devein shrimp.

Melt butter in top of double boiler. Stir in flour; gradually add half-and-half. Cook over hot water, stirring frequently, until sauce is thickened. Add paprika, 2 teaspoons salt, ¼ teaspoon white pepper, mushrooms, and shrimp. Let simmer in top of double boiler while preparing fish.

Split fillets down centers. Begin at larger end of fillet and roll it up. Fasten each with a toothpick. Place in large skillet. Add milk, water, 1 teaspoon salt, and ¼ teaspoon white pepper. Cover fish tightly; simmer gently 10 minutes.

Remove fish to hot platter; remove toothpicks and cover fish with Shrimp Sauce. Garnish with parsley before serving. Makes 8 servings.

61

polish carp

1 4-pound dressed carp
¼ cup carp blood
2 tablespoons vinegar
2 tablespoons butter
6 green spring onions, chopped
1 bay leaf
3 peppercorns
1 teaspoon salt

¼ teaspoon white pepper
1 teaspoon sugar
6 ounces malt liquor (beer)
⅓ cup crushed gingersnaps
2 tablespoons raisins
1 sprig parsley
2 medium tomatoes, cut into
  wedges

Drain blood from carp; reserve. Wash fish well under running water; dry with paper towels. Cut into serving pieces.

Mix fish blood and vinegar well; reserve.

Melt butter in skillet. Add chopped onions; sauté for 3 minutes.

Mix bay leaf, peppercorns, salt, white pepper, sugar, and beer. Cook for 20 minutes. Strain. Add blood and vinegar to strained liquid. Stir to mix. Add gingersnaps and raisins; bring to boil. Lay carp pieces in sauce; boil gently 30 minutes.

Arrange carp on serving platter. Cover with sauce; garnish with parsley and tomato wedges. Makes 4 servings.

broiled salmon steaks with herbs

4 fresh salmon steaks, ¾ inch thick
2 tablespoons grated onion
⅓ cup butter, melted
1 teaspoon salt
¼ teaspoon black pepper, peppermill-ground
½ teaspoon marjoram
1 tablespoon chopped fresh dill
2 tablespoons chopped parsley

Place salmon steaks on broiler pan.

Mix remaining ingredients; pour half of mixture over steaks. Broil 2 inches from source of heat about 4 minutes. Turn steaks. Pour remaining sauce over steaks. Return steaks to broiler; broil an additional 6 to 7 minutes or until fish flakes easily with a fork. Makes 4 servings.

pan-fried fish

6 pan-dressed fish
1 teaspoon salt
¼ teaspoon black pepper,
  peppermill-ground

2 eggs, beaten
¼ cup milk
2 cups bread crumbs
Fat for frying

Wash freshly killed fish; pan-dress. Sprinkle both sides of fish with salt and pepper.

Combine eggs and milk to form an egg wash. Dip fish in egg wash; roll them in bread crumbs.

Place fish in skillet containing ⅛ inch heated fat. Fry at moderate heat. When fish is brown on one side, turn carefully and brown remaining side. Cooking time on each side is about 10 minutes; however, the time will vary depending on size of the fish. Drain immediately on a heavy brown paper bag to remove excess grease. Makes 6 servings.

baked fish with mushroom stuffing

4-pound whole fish of your choice, dressed
1 teaspoon salt

mushroom stuffing
3 tablespoons butter
1 small onion, chopped
½ cup chopped fresh mushrooms
2 cups dry bread crumbs
¾ cup chicken stock
1 egg, beaten
½ teaspoon salt
¼ teaspoon pepper

4 strips bacon

Prepare Mushroom Stuffing. Put butter in saucepan. Add onion; sauté until onion is golden but not brown. Add chopped mushrooms; cook until water from mushrooms cooks away. Remove from heat. Add bread crumbs, chicken stock, egg, ½ teaspoon salt, and pepper. Mix well with your hands.

Clean and rub inside of fish with 1 teaspoon salt. Stuff fish. Fasten with toothpicks. Place fish, underside down, in greased baking dish. Layer bacon over top of fish. Bake in moderate (350°F) oven 1 hour or until fish flakes easily with a fork.

Remove fish to a hot platter to serve. Makes 8 servings.

lobster and rice

¼ cup butter
1 medium onion, chopped
2 cups rice
1 quart fish stock (chicken stock may be substituted)
1 bay leaf
2 tablespoons grated Parmesan cheese
2 cups cooked lobster
¼ cup sour cream
½ teaspoon salt
¼ teaspoon white pepper
¼ teaspoon paprika

Melt butter in frying pan. Add onion; cook over low heat until soft. Add rice; cook about 5 minutes, stirring constantly. Cover with stock, bring to a boil, and add bay leaf. Reduce heat, cover tightly, and steam until rice is tender. Add cheese, lobster meat, sour cream, salt, white pepper, and paprika. Makes 6 servings.

oyster soufflé

1 pint standard oysters
3 tablespoons butter
3 tablespoons flour
1 cup half-and-half
1 teaspoon salt
¼ teaspoon white pepper
3 egg yolks, beaten
3 egg whites, beaten stiff

Drain and chop oysters.

Melt butter; blend in flour until a paste forms. Add half-and-half; cook, stirring constantly, until thick. Remove from heat. Add oysters, seasonings, and beaten egg yolks.

Beat egg whites until stiff. Fold into oyster mixture. Pour mixture into greased casserole. Bake in 350°F oven 30 minutes or until brown. Makes 6 servings.

stuffed lamb chops

6 double-rib lamb chops
1 3-ounce can mushroom slices, drained
2 tablespoons mushroom liquid
1 teaspoon salt
¼ cup dry sherry wine
1 egg, beaten
½ cup bread crumbs
¼ teaspoon white pepper

Using sharp knife, make slit from bone side between rib bones into center of meat on each chop.

Drain mushrooms, reserving 2 tablespoons liquid.

Mix together reserved mushroom liquid, ½ teaspoon salt, sherry, beaten egg, mushrooms, and bread crumbs. Stuff chops with mushroom mixture. Sprinkle with remaining ½ teaspoon salt and pepper. Broil lamb chops 4 to 5 inches from flame, 12 minutes on each side.

Serve immediately. Makes 6 servings.

dilled lamb chops

1 tablespoon butter
4 blade lamb chops, ½ inch thick
1 can condensed cream of mushroom soup
½ cup water
1 teaspoon ground dillseed

Melt butter in large skillet. Add lamb chops; brown evenly on both sides.

Combine soup, water, and dillseed; mix well. Add to skillet containing lamb chops. Cover skillet; simmer for 35 to 40 minutes, stirring occasionally, until lamb chops are fork-tender. Makes 4 servings.

lamb in sour-cream sauce

3 tablespoons butter
3 pounds lamb shoulder, cut into 1-inch cubes
1 tablespoon salt
½ teaspoon black pepper, peppermill-ground
2 tablespoons paprika
2 onions, sliced thin
1 cup hot water
2 cups sour cream
1 pound egg noodles
1 tablespoon poppy seeds

Melt butter in large Dutch oven. Add lamb cubes; brown evenly. Drain drippings from lamb cubes. Sprinkle cubes with salt, pepper, and paprika. Add onions and water, cover, and simmer 1 hour or until lamb is tender. Add more water during cooking period if needed. Gradually stir in sour cream; heat but do not boil.

While meat is cooking, cook noodles according to package directions; drain. Add poppy seeds to noodles; toss.

To serve, arrange noodles on a serving platter. Pour lamb and sauce over noodles. Makes 8 servings.

polish sausage cooked in molasses

1½ quarts cold water
⅓ cup molasses
1 teaspoon dry mustard
1½ pounds Polish sausage

Combine water, molasses, and dry mustard in large saucepan. Bring mixture to rapid boil. Add Polish sausage. Cover. Reduce heat to simmer. Cook sausage until heated thoroughly, approximately 15 minutes per pound. While sausage is still in cooking liquid, puncture casing with a fork to reduce pressure inside casing,

Remove sausage from water and slice into serving pieces. Serve immediately. Makes 4 servings.

kielbasa pockets

¼ cup butter, melted
1 teaspoon prepared mustard
1 package crescent rolls
1 pound Kielbasa (Polish sausage)

Combine melted butter and prepared mustard. Stir until mustard is blended into the butter.

Unwrap package of rolls; carefully separate dough into 8 pieces. Brush each piece with some of butter and mustard mixture.

Cut Polish sausage crosswise into 8 equal pieces. Place sausage on dough pieces; roll dough around sausages, being sure to start rolling on wide end of dough. Place rolled sausage on ungreased baking sheet, placing exposed seam on the bottom. Brush tops of dough with remaining butter and mustard mixture. Bake in preheated 350°F oven 15 minutes.

Serve Kielbasa immediately. Makes 4 servings.

polish links in sauerkraut

Try this delicious dish for a quick lunch.

2 cups sauerkraut
1 tablespoon caraway seed
¼ cup beer
8 Polish links (hot dogs may be substituted)
8 hot dog buns, warmed
¼ cup finely chopped onions
Mustard

Combine sauerkraut, caraway seed, beer, and Polish links in large saucepan. Bring mixture to a boil, reduce heat to simmer, and cook for 30 minutes.

To serve, place Polish links in buns and top with ¼ cup sauerkraut. Garnish with chopped onions and mustard. Makes 4 servings.

ham hocks in sauerkraut

Delicious served with boiled potatoes and rye bread.

3 large ham hocks
2 cups sauerkraut
1 large onion, sliced into thin rings
1 tablespoon granulated sugar
¼ teaspoon black pepper

Cover ham hocks with water; simmer for 1 hour. Drain.

Add sauerkraut, onion, sugar, and pepper to ham hocks. Return to heat; simmer 1½ to 2 hours or until meat falls off the bone. Makes 4 servings.

noodles and ham

3 tablespoons butter
2 tablespoons all-purpose white flour
1 cup half-and-half
1 cup shredded cheddar cheese
1 tablespoon prepared horseradish
1 cup cooked peas
2 cups diced cooked ham
1½ cups cooked noodles
¼ cup dry bread crumbs

Melt 2 tablespoons butter in a saucepan. Blend flour into melted butter to form a paste. Add milk, stirring constantly until a smooth, thick sauce forms. Add cheese; stir sauce until cheese melts. Add horseradish, peas, ham, and noodles; blend well.

Pour mixture into a greased 1-quart casserole dish. Top meat and noodle mixture with bread crumbs; dot with remaining 1 tablespoon butter. Bake casserole in 350°F oven 30 minutes or until heated thoroughly. Makes 4 servings.

pork chops with cabbage and potatoes

4 medium-size potatoes
2 teaspoons salt
1 small head cabbage
¼ cup oil
8 ¼-inch pork chops
¼ teaspoon white pepper

Peel and quarter potatoes. Place potatoes in 3-quart saucepan. Sprinkle with 1 teaspoon salt; cover with cold water. Bring potatoes and water to a boil. Reduce heat; simmer for 10 minutes.

Shred cabbage; add to potatoes. Cook for 10 to 15 minutes or until cabbage and potatoes are tender. Drain.

While vegetables are cooking, fry pork chops in oil until brown and well-done. Drain. Reserve ¼ cup of oil and drippings in which pork chops were fried.

Place potatoes and cabbage in center of large serving tray. Pour reserved oil and drippings over vegetables. Sprinkle with ¼ teaspoon white pepper and 1 teaspoon salt. Arrange pork chops around outer rim of serving tray. Serve immediately. Makes 4 servings.

Picture on opposite page: ham hocks in sauerkraut

pork steak
in wine sauce

2 tablespoons vegetable shortening
4 1-inch-thick pork steaks
½ cup finely chopped onions
1 cup sliced fresh mushrooms
1 cup red wine
1 sprig parsley
2 Dilled Tomato Cups with Peas (see Index)

Heat a brazier or large frying pan, add 2 tablespoons vegetable shortening, and stir until melted. Add pork steaks; brown on both sides. Remove meat from skillet.

Add onions and mushrooms to skillet. Continue cooking until vegetables are wilted but not browned. Re-add steaks to skillet. Pour wine over steaks. Cover tightly; simmer about 1 hour or until steaks are fork-tender.

To serve, arrange steaks on serving platter. Garnish with parsley and Dilled Tomato Cups with Peas. Makes 4 servings.

Picture on previous pages: pork steak in wine sauce

desserts

cottage-cheese and pear stacks

1 1-pound can pear halves
1 cup all-purpose white flour
½ teaspoon baking soda
¼ teaspoon salt
2 tablespoons granulated sugar

1 egg, beaten
1 cup sour milk
⅓ cup butter, melted
2 cups small-curd cottage cheese

Drain pear halves, reserving liquid for Marmalade Sauce.

Combine flour, baking soda, salt, and sugar.

Blend egg and milk; beat into flour mixture until smooth.

Pour 1 tablespoon butter into 5½-inch skillet. Add enough batter to cover bottom of pan; brown on both sides. Repeat, using remaining batter. Stack pancakes, spreading cottage cheese between each layer.

Arrange pear quarters, fan-shape, on top of stack. Cut in wedges; serve with Marmalade Sauce. Makes 6 servings.

marmalade sauce

¾ cup pear syrup
1 cup orange marmalade
1 tablespoon cornstarch
¼ teaspoon mace

Combine all ingredients. Cook until thickened. Serve over Cottage-Cheese and Pear Stacks. Makes 1¾ cups.

hot-water chocolate cake

2 cups granulated sugar
2 cups all-purpose white flour
¼ cup cocoa
½ teaspoon salt
1 teaspoon soda

½ cup butter
1 cup water
½ cup sour milk
2 eggs, beaten
1 teaspoon vanilla

Combine sugar, flour, cocoa, salt, and soda. Set aside.

Bring butter and water to boil. Remove from heat; stir in dry ingredients. Add milk, eggs, and vanilla; mix thoroughly.

Pour cake batter into greased 9 × 13-inch pan. Bake at 375°F for 25 minutes or until a toothpick inserted into center comes out clean. Remove cake from oven; frost immediately with Chocolate Frosting. Makes 24 servings.

chocolate frosting

⅓ cup half-and-half
½ cup butter
⅓ cup cocoa

1 pound powdered sugar
1 teaspoon vanilla
½ cup English walnuts

Combine half-and-half, butter, and cocoa in saucepan. Bring to boil. Add powdered sugar and vanilla; beat until blended. Stir in English walnuts. Spread on cake while frosting and cake are still warm.

cinnamon cake

¾ cup butter
1 cup granulated sugar
1 egg
1½ teaspoons cinnamon

1½ cups all-purpose white flour
1½ cups whipping cream
1 teaspoon vanilla

Cream butter until soft. Gradually add ¾ cup sugar; beat until light and fluffy. Add egg; beat well. Add cinnamon and flour; mix well. Spread about ⅓ of batter on ungreased baking sheet into a rectangle about 10 × 12 inches. Bake in 400°F oven 8 minutes or until lightly browned. Remove from oven; let stand a few minutes. Cut cake into 3 equal rectangles; transfer to cooling rack.

Repeat process with remaining batter.

Whip cream until stiff. Fold in ¼ cup sugar and vanilla. Spread a thin layer of whipped cream between each piece of cake. Top with remaining cream; serve immediately. Makes 8 servings.

vanilla ice cream

½ cup granulated sugar
4 egg yolks
2 cups half-and-half
2 cups whipping cream
2 teaspoons vanilla

Mix sugar and egg yolks in top of double boiler. Pour half-and-half on top of egg-yolk mixture. Cook egg-yolk and half-and-half mixture in double boiler until mixture coats spoon. Cool and strain. Add cream and vanilla. Freeze in conventional ice-cream freezer. Makes 1½ quarts.

rice pudding with sour cream

1½ cups cold water
1 cup whole milk
1 teaspoon salt
1 cup uncooked rice
1 cup seedless raisins
2 tablespoons butter

2 tablespoons granulated sugar
½ teaspoon nutmeg
1 cup sour cream
¼ cup sugar
1 teaspoon vanilla extract

Combine 1 cup cold water, milk, salt, and uncooked rice in 3-quart saucepan. Place on heated surface; bring mixture to boil. Stir rice once; cover. Turn heat very low; cook for 20 minutes or until water and milk are absorbed. Do not lift lid during cooking.

While rice is cooking, combine remaining ½ cup cold water and raisins. Simmer for 10 minutes or until raisins have absorbed their cooking water.

Combine cooked rice and raisins. Blend in butter, 2 tablespoons sugar, and nutmeg. Mix well. Pour rice pudding into greased 1-quart mold. Chill.

In chilled bowl, whip sour cream until it stands in soft peaks. Blend in ¼ cup sugar and vanilla. Be careful not to overwhip the sour cream, or butter will result. To serve pudding, slice and top with whipped sour cream. Makes 8 servings.

cheesecake

18 ounces cream cheese
⅔ cup zwieback crumbs, packed
1 teaspoon vanilla

5 egg whites
1 cup granulated sugar
1 can fruit pie filling

Let cream cheese stand at room temperature until softened.

Sprinkle bottom and sides of buttered 8-inch springform pan with zwieback crumbs, pressing any extra crumbs evenly on bottom of pan.

Put cream cheese into mixing bowl. Add vanilla; cream until fluffy.

Beat egg whites until foamy. Beat in sugar, ⅓ cup at a time, beating well after each addition. Beat until whites are stiff enough to hold a peak but not dry. Fold gently into cheese. Turn mixture into springform pan lined with zwieback. Bake at 350°F for 25 minutes. Remove from oven (center will still be soft); let cool away from drafts. When cake is room temperature, chill in refrigerator 4 hours.

Remove side of pan. Cut into serving pieces; garnish with fruit filling. Makes 12 servings.

baba au rum

½ cup milk
⅓ cup butter
1 teaspoon salt
1¼ cups granulated sugar
1 package active dry yeast
¼ cup warm water
2 eggs, beaten

½ teaspoon grated lemon peel
2¼ cups all-purpose white flour
½ cup water
½ cup molasses
½ cup rum
½ cup powdered sugar

Scald milk; add butter, salt, and ¼ cup granulated sugar until melted. Cool to lukewarm.

Dissolve yeast in warm water. Add to lukewarm milk; mix well. Stir in beaten eggs and lemon peel. Add flour; beat until smooth. Cover; let rise for 5 hours. Beat down until smooth and elastic.

Fill greased tube pan or Baba mold. Let dough rise uncovered 30 minutes. Bake in 425°F oven 20 minutes or until done. Remove from pan at once.

Combine ½ cup water, 1 cup sugar, and molasses in heavy saucepan. Bring mixture to boil; boil rapidly 10 minutes. Cool mixture slightly; add rum.

Place Baba in serving dish; soak with rum sauce 24 hours prior to serving.

To serve, dust Baba with powdered sugar. Makes 12 servings.

almond torte

6 egg yolks
1 cup granulated sugar
1 teaspoon grated lemon rind
2 tablespoons lemon juice
1 teaspoon cinnamon

1 cup ground almonds
¾ cup fine bread crumbs
6 egg whites
¼ teaspoon salt

Beat egg yolks until thick and light in color. Gradually beat in sugar; continue beating until light and fluffy. Add lemon rind, juice, cinnamon, almonds, and bread crumbs; blend well.

Whip egg whites and salt until stiff. Fold egg whites carefully into yolk mixture. Pour into greased 8-inch tube pan; bake in 350°F oven 1 hour. Remove from oven; let cool in pan. Makes 8 servings.

crepe batter

3 eggs, beaten
1½ teaspoons granulated sugar
1¾ cups milk
1½ cups all-purpose white flour

3 tablespoons butter, melted
1 teaspoon vanilla
½ cup butter, melted

Beat eggs until frothy. Combine with sugar and milk; gradually beat into flour. Add 3 tablespoons melted butter and vanilla; beat smooth. (Batter should be quite thin.) Heat 1 tablespoon butter in heavy 5-inch skillet. Pour in just enough batter to cover bottom of pan. Cook until bubbles appear and underside is browned. Turn or flip; lightly brown other side. Continue to make crepes, heating a teaspoon of butter to sizzling for each crepe.

Serve crepes with your favorite sauce. Makes 2 dozen crepes.

baba au rum

cottage-cheese-filled crepes

cottage-cheese-filled crepes

1 recipe Crepe Batter (see Index)
1½ cups dry-curd cottage cheese
1 teaspoon cinnamon
2 egg yolks, beaten
2 tablespoons granulated sugar
1 teaspoon vanilla
3 tablespoons kirsch
¼ cup powdered sugar

Prepare crepes as directed. Keep them warm.

Rub cottage cheese through a seive. Mix with cinnamon, egg yolks, granulated sugar, vanilla, and kirsch.

Fill crepes with cottage-cheese mixture; roll them up.

To serve, place crepes on warm serving dish; dust with powdered sugar. Makes 2 dozen crepes.

polish easter cake

½ cup milk
½ cup granulated sugar
½ teaspoon salt
¼ cup butter
¼ cup warm water
1 package active dry yeast
2 eggs, beaten
2½ cups all-purpose white flour
½ cup chopped almonds
½ cup raisins
½ teaspoon lemon peel
1 cup confectioners' sugar
1 tablespoon milk
Whole candied cherries

Scald milk. Stir in sugar, salt, and butter. Cool to lukewarm.

Pour lukewarm water into large bowl. Sprinkle yeast over water; stir until dissolved. Add milk mixture, eggs, and flour; beat vigorously 5 minutes. Cover; let rise in warm place, free from draft, for 1½ hours or until doubled in bulk. Stir batter down; beat in almonds, raisins, and lemon peel. Pour batter into greased and floured 1½-quart casserole. Let rise for 1 hour. Bake in 350°F oven 50 minutes. Let cool in pan 20 minutes before removing.

Beat together 1 cup confectioners' sugar and 1 tablespoon milk to form glaze.

To serve, place cake on serving platter; drizzle glaze on top. Garnish with cherries. Makes 8 servings.

polish easter cake

sugar and spice rice

sugar and spice rice

1 cup cold water
1 cup whole milk
1 teaspoon salt
1 cup uncooked rice
½ cup butter
½ cup granulated sugar
2 teaspoons cinnamon

Combine water, milk, salt, and uncooked rice in 3-quart saucepan. Bring mixture to boil. Stir rice once; cover. Turn heat very low; cook for 20 minutes or until water and milk are absorbed. Do not uncover while cooking.

Spoon rice into serving dishes; top each serving with 2 tablespoons butter, 2 tablespoons sugar, and ½ teaspoon cinnamon. Serve immediately. Makes 4 servings.

warsaw party torte

warsaw party torte

½ pound almonds, ground	3 teaspoons vanilla
6 tablespoons all-purpose white flour	10 egg whites
1 teaspoon cream of tartar	3 cups whipping cream
10 egg yolks	1 cup slivered almonds, toasted
1¾ cups granulated sugar	12 fresh red raspberries

Combine ground almonds, flour, and cream of tarter.

Beat egg yolks until light and fluffy. Gradually beat 1¼ cups sugar into egg yolks; continue to beat until mixture is thick and smooth. Stir in 1 teaspoon vanilla. Fold in flour mixture.

Beat egg whites until very stiff. Fold egg whites into egg-yolk mixture.

Line bottom of 10-inch tube pan with wax paper. Pour batter into pan. Bake in 375°F oven 1 hour or until done. Invert cake; cool thoroughly. Remove from pan.

Whip cream, adding ½ cup granulated sugar and 2 teaspoons vanilla at end of whipping period.

Place cake, top-side-down, on serving platter; cover center hole with small plastic or cardboard disk. Frost cake with whipped cream. Using pastry tube, decorate edge with whipped-cream flowers. Press toasted almonds around sides of frosted cake. Garnish each whipped-cream flower with a fresh raspberry.

Refrigerate torte prior to serving. Makes 12 servings.

index